CONDUCTING THE EXPERIENTIAL GROUP

An Introduction to Group Dynamics

John M. Toothman

University Press of America,® Inc.
Lanham · New York · Oxford

**Copyright © 2000 by
University Press of America,® Inc.**
4720 Boston Way
Lanham, Maryland 20706

12 Hid's Copse Rd.
Cumnor Hill, Oxford OX2 9JJ

British Library Cataloging in Publication Information Available

Library of Congress Cataloging-in-Publication Data

Toothman. John.
Conducting the experimental group : an introduction to group
dynamics / John M. Toothman.
p.   cm.
Includes bibliographical references.
1. Social groups. 2. Communication in small groups. 3. Group
relations training. I. Title.
HM716 .T66   2000   302.3'4—dc21   00-046726 CIP

ISBN 0-7618-1858-8 (pbk : alk. paper)

CONTENTS

THE AUTHOR

John M. Toothman is an Associate Professor of Psychology at Goldey-Beacom College in Wilmington, Delaware. For 12 years, he was the lead Professor for Human Communication Groups offered by Eastern Washington University for the United States Air Force. He conducted groups in Germany, Portugal, Korea, Philippines, Guam, and Hawaii. Dr. Toothman holds a Ph.D. in Human Behavior from United States International University and is presently involved in developing excellence in his Group Dynamics Course at Goldey-Beacom College.

PREFACE

This book is designed to provide a basic reference for both the group member and the group leader who might be in need of understanding and conducting a small group experience. It is meant to be used for the basic understanding of the subject matter of group processes and as a stimulus for the group leader as well as the participant. The format is designed to give clarity to the often nebulous field of group dynamics.

Considerable emphasis is placed on the role of experiential groups as an educational tool, and, quite possibly, even a vehicle for personal and social change. The direction offered has the tendency to suggest a developmental phase model of group dynamics, but, at the same time, encourages group leaders to make their own experiential groups as unique as possible. The format allows for group leaders to be creative in their use of designs and techniques.

INTRODUCTION TO GROUP DYNAMICS

Group dynamics usually refers to the study of individuals interacting in small groups. Kurt Lewin's work at the Massachusetts Institute of Technology which included books such as A Dynamic Theory of Personality (1935) and Resolving Social Conflicts (1948) helped establish group dynamics as a tool that could be used for teaching people how to change ideas as well as social behavior. He found that when people were allowed to work in a laboratory group, most people learned something about their own behavior in groups and developed insights into the group dynamics process. From Lewin's pioneering work on the group laboratory method of learning came the field of group dynamics, and its use in the academic disciplines of psychology, sociology, organizational development, and human resources, along with use in fields that include management, labor organization, business enterprises, and the military.

Two organizations have been responsible for the continued development of the group dynamics process. The National Training Laboratories (NTL) in 1951 began a program of experiential learning in human relations groups (T-Groups) with the objective being personal growth, interpersonal communication skills, and possibly behavioral change. The Tavistock Institute of Human Relations in England was responsible for influencing and teaching the group dynamics process in Europe.

Organizations are constantly bombarded by the problems associated with getting seemingly competent people to work together. For example, the CEO of a major corporation cannot understand why his or her executive staff cannot get along, even when their working conditions and salaries are the same. The United States Armed Forces are constantly in search of ways to get their supervisory staff better equipped to motivate a new work force with often different points of view. Business executives, military leaders, and educational managers are often not sure just how to teach and direct leadership.

The goal of group dynamics is to bring intervention strategies to give clearer insights into managerial and organizational dilemmas. Many of the often-misunderstood dynamics involving the human experience can often be understood through the use of the small group experience. Group experience can have not only personal benefit, but can have a profound effect on the behavior and attitude of management and the individual workers. Supervisors can often learn about their own particular personality as participants in an experiential group process. As a result, they are often able to address the problem issues and take the beginning steps to solve them. Lewin and Butler (1952) found greater effectiveness of learning in the group process over a direct-line, do-as-I-say methodology. Many people can work well with others, but when problems or difficulties occur, there are often few ways to resolve the issues. Group dynamics, like other social management sciences, offers the experiential group process as the vehicle for examining behavior in relationships to others. People bring their basic personality into groups, and the purpose of the group dynamics process is to help each group member define and understand his or her particular group behavior.

The overall group dynamics process is based on the idea that the small group experience is a distinct process that deals with emotions and personalities. Lewin (1944) felt that the field of group dynamics, if properly handled, could strengthen a rational approach to our social problems more than any other social science field. Group dynamics means trying to understand the interaction of group members and formulating a series of possible ideas about what the behavior signifies.

Chapter 1

UNDERSTANDING THE PURPOSE OF EXPERIENTIAL GROUP DYNAMICS

The purpose of experiential group dynamics is to learn behavioral processes so that the individual group members may better understand all kinds of groups. Group dynamics seminars differ considerably from group psychotherapy, and it is important to understand some of the differences. In group psychotherapy the patient (group member) suffers from mild to severe maladaptive conditions, whereas the experiential group dynamics participant is essentially a fairly normal individual who wants to improve his or her interpersonal communication skills and overall knowledge of working with other people. In group therapy, unconscious conflicts are often dealt with by searching for the origins of these attitudes. In experiential group dynamics, the focus is on the "here and now" and deep unconscious conflicts are not analyzed or examined. The experiential group is designed around the learning of ideas and concepts, with movement toward cognitive and behavioral changes. These ideas are supported by the National Training Laboratories. This experiential process can be an excellent method for gaining new insights towards one's relationship with others.

Experiential groups get most of their working framework from phases developed by developmental psychologist Erik Erikson (1963). Erikson felt that it was necessary to resolve the conflicts from one stage before one could move on to the next conflict stage. This process helps provide an order and understanding to the experiential group process. Group sessions, readings, written assignments, and lecture material can all be used in support of the developmental phase.

The developmental process often does not take an ideal sequence. Regression or lack of resolution of a phase may prevent movement through all the phases. Regardless of the success or failure of the small group experience, there will be a defined beginning and ending.

In summary, the experiential group learning process attempts to meet some of the following criteria:

- becomes a self-regulating system,
- searches for feedback patterns,
- studies the present (here and now),
- studies exploration and creativity,
- studies interpersonal communication dynamics,
- interacts with the environment and the work world,
- studies group processes and their relationships to larger systems,
- searches for present patterns of interaction, and
- creates cognitive/behavioral changes.

Chapter 2

STARTING THE EXPERIENTIAL GROUP EXPERIENCE

In every group experience I have undertaken, the big question has always been, "How do I get started?" "How do I get people involved or interested in the small group experience?" The best approach I have found in interpreting the group experience to new members is to point out that through the group experience members can acquire an understanding of interpersonal relationships with other group members as well as with people in every day life.

Group members learn to help others adapt as well as themselves. The group experience provides an opportunity to have others point out things they cannot see in themselves since the common tendency is to lose one's own objectivity. We seldom see ourselves as others do. The new member is assured that all members of the group are experiencing the same emotional stress and life-in-general problems. In addition, the group experience will be similar in many ways to group relationships met in everyday life and working environments.

Alderfer (1995), in presenting conditions for teaching experiential group dynamics, recommends a pre-group interview to establish purpose and direction. This is extremely important for undergraduate and graduate students studying group dynamics because they are bound by the rules of the academic process. The group experience cannot be a part of the grade evaluation; therefore, "right" or "wrong" answers would not be a basis for grades. Whether the group is composed of college students or mid-level managers, the goal of the pre-interview is to establish the importance of how a group member's behavior is perceived by others.

The relationship established in this pre-group interview sets the stage for the group climate that will exist and the commitment to the group that the member will have.

Technical Considerations

The concerns that usually arise in starting a new group are things such as the meeting place, the frequency and the duration of the meetings, the number of members, whether or not visitors will be allowed, the use of limits, etc.

Meeting Place

Removing the group members from their usual surroundings and social pressures is advocated by numerous group dynamics theorists. A setting of this nature is often preferred, but it is not always possible for practical reasons. In the institutional setting, the place of the meeting is pretty well solved. The important part is that the setting is relatively free of distractions and reasonably quiet. Ventilation is, of course, important, and there should be sufficient light so that everyone is seen clearly in the group. It is generally felt that a group seated in a circle, without tables or other barriers between them, is best able to facilitate free interaction and discussion in the group. Studies by Hare and Bales (1963) found the interaction occurred more frequently between members who sat opposite each other then those who were sitting adjacent.

Recording

Some experiential groups make use of both audio and visual recordings of the group process. This method is often used in academic groups where students are evaluated for their analytical work on the group process. If it is used for research purposes or for feedback for future group meetings, it might have some value. For example, in affording the group an opportunity to evaluate its own behavioral progress. In no instance should a recording be made without the knowledge of the group. Aside from the ethical violation, it could betray the trust of each group member. Before any recording is done, it is necessary to consider the nature of the individuals in the group, whether or not recording will increase self-consciousness, inhibit response, or defeat the original purpose of the experiential group.

Frequency and Duration of Meetings

In many organizations and institutional settings the frequency of group sessions is often regulated administratively, in line with the schedule of other activities within the facility. Generally speaking, the frequency of meetings should reflect the pace at which the group is proceeding. The frequency can often be altered if necessary. In most settings groups meet once or twice a week.

The maximum meeting time for experiential groups is three hours. Some suggest a flexible program, while others feel that there should be a rigidity about the time. Extending time is often impossible with students of group dynamics classes and can create administrative problems within the organizational community.

Group Size

The ideal group size for experiential groups is 15 to 20, with 25 being the absolute limit. The larger size groups have a tendency to break down into smaller groups, which limits the opportunity for individual expression. The group leader should have plenty of group activities that can accommodate the sub-group level.

Open Versus Closed Groups

An open group is one where new members are added as old members leave. This type of group is often mandatory in organizational settings as employees change jobs, move on, etc. This can often help the group process with the introduction of new ideas and these new members can often break cliques, thereby creating a greater social growth of the group. The greatest advantage of a closed group is that the members develop closer ties and can continue to develop the experiential/analytical connection because the group is not slowed down by the assimilation of new members.

The Mandatory Group Requirement

Can a meaningful group experience develop from mandatory participation? Yes, even involuntary participation is a starting point for some significant life changes. For example, a group member's acceptance of responsibility for his or her own behavior can lead to a much improved working situation. However, the reluctant group member can place tremendous pressure on the group leader, and in many ways, this is where the ability or lack of ability of the group leader is often tested.

Basic Group Rules

In working with experiential groups, it is important to set certain rules (guidelines for group behavior) at the beginning of the first session. Usually these guidelines are introduced as a part of the group leader's orientation session.

Among group theorists there is considerable differences regarding group rules and how these rules are to be enforced. There are group leaders who prefer no limits whatsoever, and in some group experiences, this works quite well. I have been able to use a no-limits approach quite successfully with military human relations training groups and also in my undergraduate and graduate group dynamics classes. If, for example, one or more of the participants were talking and the group was becoming chaotic, all I needed to do was point out the confusion and how hard it is to listen to more than one person talking at a time. This usually leads to a group discussion of how this can be handled, and, as a result, the group as a whole would help set the limits. However, much more control could be used by the group leader. A statement should be made as to a rule that only one person can talk at a time. These two approaches more than likely would produce the same results and keep the group moving toward growth and change.

Generally, there are limits that often have to be established. Time, physical expression against another group member, and group attendance are important issues to be addressed in the orientation session. A good rule of thumb is that a group member will be dropped from the group should his or her attendance become irregular without justification. In my group dynamics classes, I make regular attendance a requirement to get an acceptable grade for the course. The group leader needs to give group members a clear view of limitations before the start of the group sessions.

Language

Since socially acceptable language is necessary in the larger context of life, I find it more comfortable to express the desire for some controls on abusive or socially unacceptable language (i.e., slang, non-complimentary nicknames, vulgarities, and swearing). There are other group leaders who would disagree with the type of control and feel that controlling language is curtailing expression.

Group leaders need to establish their own approach and define any limits at the beginning. It is important to remember that one of the purposes of the experiential group is to build the self-esteem of each group member, and this can be accomplished by eliminating derogatory expression of feelings.

Guests

Strangers (guests) are usually disruptive to the experiential group process and can slow down the group process itself. In extreme cases, it could possibly stop the group process. Under no circumstances should guests be permitted without the knowledge and consent of the group members.

Physical Activities

An absolute rule for experiential groups is that physically aggressive interactions is unacceptable behavior. Leaving the room, roaming about, reading, singing, whistling, etc. are all considered disruptive to the growth of the group process and should be avoided if possible.

Record Keeping

There is wide variation in the practice of keeping some type of records of the group sessions. Some make video films, while others keep almost verbatim accounts of their sessions. Group leaders need to decide if detailed accounts are necessary for research and training purposes. In most standard experiential groups, detailed accounts are often not necessary. A written summary will often meet the requirements for reference material for management record keeping. Group theorists usually recommend a written summary of the basic theme of each group session.

The Issue of Confidentiality

Confidentiality is very hard to enforce. It is only natural for group members to want to continue their discussions following the group session. It takes a while for group members to make the distinction between behavior in group as opposed to behavior at work or at school. Even though it is almost impossible to stop outside activity, it is important that the group leader stresses the importance and need for confidentiality. Hopefully, as a result, they will develop a respect for the importance of confidentiality issues.

Cancellation of the Group

It is important for the group leader to be present once the group process has been established. The transference relationship has usually occurred with a personal investment in the group leader by the group members. Therefore the group session should be canceled if the group leader is unable to be present for that session.

Chapter 3

FACTORS IN EXPERIENTIAL GROUPS

An experiential group should be able to provide both an intellectual and psychological stimulating experience. The purpose is to get group members to create a greater awareness of who they are, while at the same time increase the possibility of some behavioral change.

Some of the factors that occur in groups which must be dealt with by the group leader are often described by group theorists as transference, disorganization, group tension, resistance, group monopolizer, acting out, non-verbal communication, and group and individual silence.

Transference

In 1909 Sigmund Freud made the observation that transference arises spontaneously in all human relationships. He felt that transference occurs when a person automatically projects in the authority figure (group leader) many of his or her irrational thoughts and conflicts. Interpretation and group discussion of transference is often the major tool for facilitating behavioral change in the experiential group. Often the group itself will provide the necessary framework for the needed support to bring out numerous unresolved interpersonal conflicts.

Resistance

Resistance in the experiential group process is quite often interpreted as a resistance to behavioral change. A group member's personality that has been threatened or interfered with will, as a result, be somewhat fearful of any type of self-disclosure. Resistance to the group process can be a way of warding off the accompanying anxiety. The role of the group leader is to be aware of the importance of developing a group structure that encourages a trusting environment for expression of thoughts, feelings, goals, etc.

Resistance in groups can be directly observed through peripheral involvement, tardiness, intellectualization of subject matter, expressed hostility, silence, boredom, and impulsive (acting-out) behavior.

The Group Monopolizer

The group member who often uses his or her intellectual ability in a defensive manner tends to contribute to the inhibition of the group process. Usually these members are sophisticated enough to know that as long as they are in control, the issues that they find threatening cannot be raised by others. Since this type of behavior is extremely detrimental to the overall group process, it is important for the group leader to assist the group itself in identifying ways to handle the monopolist(s). This involves helping group members examine their own feelings and behaviors and finding solutions for moving on in the group process.

Acting Out

Acting out can occur in the experiential group and is, in many ways, to be expected. There is usually a high degree of socially acceptable behavior in this type of group experience, but like any other group, the experiential group can cause considerable anxiety. Acting-out behavior, however, can be used constructively by calling attention to the behavior and have the group make it a part of its group process. The group leader can be very helpful in encouraging the group to work through hostile feelings rather than have the group members express them in indirect ways.

Non-Verbal Communication

It is important for the group leader to be aware of contradictory communication. It is not all too common for group members to express an emotion verbally while non-verbally expressing a different message, i.e., stating anger while smiling. Group leaders need to be aware of the double messages presented by the various gestures, body movements, and facial expressions as they accompany verbal communications. The group process can be enhanced by having the group deal with these contradictory messages as they develop.

Absences and Late Arrival

Among group theorists, it is agreed that those who terminate the group experience prematurely derive little, if any, benefit from the experience. At the same time, their short stay can often hinder the group development process. Proper orientation is an excellent safeguard against attendance problems. Without the mandatory attendance rule, the group process runs the risk of not becoming strong enough for learning, let alone behavioral change to take place. Yalom (1966) found that inadequate orientation was one of the major categories emerging as a reason for failure of the overall group process. I have found that if group members can go beyond the third or fourth session, they will usually stay with the group. Feelings of belongingness can become very strong by the third or fourth session, and as a result, the group member wants to be a part of the group development.

Individual and Group Silences

Silent members can be a potential problem for group development. Again the group leader needs to create a climate that suggests to the silent member that he or she can get involved in the group process at any time. Silent members have a tendency to fear that what they have to say is of little importance and could be met by criticism from other group members. Structured group exercises can be very beneficial in helping the silent member begin his or her group involvement. Set activities and a plan on the part of the group leader takes away much of the self-exposure anxiety. Usually these activities provide a non-threatening environment that allows enough time for both the active and non-active group member to feel comfortable. Even if the silent members continue their non-active roles, they can still feel a part of the group process through the structured activities.

Group silence can also create considerable discomfort. Experiential groups often experience group silence at times. This often happens when the group leader attempts to move the group development away from structured experiences. In many ways, it is a way of testing the strength of the group development. Silences often indicate that the development has not reached that phase where the group is ready to engage in self-directed behavior. Often additional structure and time can be very helpful in alleviating group silence as it occurs from time to time.

Group Development

Lifton (1961) has listed the following characteristics as typical of a mature group, and they might serve as a useful measure against which group leaders may evaluate their own experiential groups:

1. an ever increasing ability to be self-directed (not dependent on leader),
2. an increased tolerance in accepting that progress takes time,
3. an increasing sensitivity to one's own feelings and the feelings of others,
4. marked improvement in the ability to withstand tension, frustration, and disagreement,
5. perception of the common denominators which bind the group, as well as areas of individual differences,

6. better ability to anticipate realistic results of behavior and to channel emotions into more socially acceptable ways of expressing these emotions,
7. an increased ability to change plans and methods as new situations develop,
8. less time needed to recover from threatening group situations--peaks and valleys of emotional group crises become less pronounced,
9. increased efficiency in locating problems, engaging in problem solving, and providing help to individuals as needed,
10. prestige in group now comes from willingness to face one's responsibilities and to assist others when help is needed,
11. acceptance of the right of the other person to be different, and
12. acceptance of the idea that people are different.

Group Composition

There are many different approaches to group composition. When working with the military/industrial world where the group experience is often required, everyone could and can be involved. In some situations, it can be a reluctant participant and often requires a strong orientation as to the "rhyme and reason" for the group experience by the group leader. This again emphasizes the importance of a very strong orientation session.

In the academic world, group dynamics classes will hopefully provide an educational experience and possibly some behavioral insights or changes for the student. Leopold (1957) suggests that potential group members should have (1) a fairly full sense of reality, (2) the capacity for being reached emotionally in an interpersonal relationship, (3) sufficient flexibility to increase or reduce intragroup tensions, and (4) the ability to act as a catalyst from time to time. Most group theorists agree that group membership would be unsuitable for members with the following personality characteristics:

1. insufficient reality contact,
2. chronic impulsive (acting-out) behavior,
3. those showing culturally deviant symptomatology,
4. extremely self-absorbed individuals,
5. chronic monopolists, and
6. suicidal individuals.

If the group leader has some control over the selection process, I would recommend screening perspective members for the following characteristics:

1. has at least a basic grasp of reality--ruling out the extremely withdrawn participant,
2. a participant who is extremely hostile and aggressive--a low threshold for impulsive behavior (acting out),
3. the seriously depressed participant,
4. impaired intellectual ability,
5. shows questionable super-ego development problems--sociopathic personalities,
6. has troublesome verbal skills, and
7. has the inability to meet affiliation needs.

These seven categories are extremely important. After all, group learning has a lot to do with the members ability to relate to each other, and at the same time, be able to analyze the experiences. With these exceptions, group theorists subscribe to the concept that the more representative of the general population the group is, the more effective it can be in the terms of relearning and offering experiences in new and often more rewarding ways of interacting. I often hear group members say that one of the biggest learning experiences is that they realize they are not alone in their thoughts and problems in life.

Chapter 4

WHAT MAKES THE EXPERIENTIAL GROUP EXPERIENCE WORK?

Considerable research has been conducted in the pursuit of answering the following question: What is it in the group approach that brings about improvement in the individual and, quite possibly, in the organization?

Corsini and Rosenberg (1955) undertook to answer this question, made a survey of the literature, and published their findings in the Journal of Abnormal and Social Psychology. They listed the mechanisms operating in groups that were offered by authors in over 300 articles or books. By clustering the most frequently appearing mechanisms and eliminating those that seemed merely to be semantically different, they came up with ten effective classic mechanisms which seemed to be operating in group

situations. Nine of these could be assigned specific labels
as follows:

1. Acceptance
2. Ventilation
3. Reality Testing
4. Transference
5. Intellectualization
6. Interaction
7. Universalization
8. Altruism
9. Spectator Learning

Acceptance

This is the feeling that one is part of and belongs to
the group and that other members will interact in a friendly,
nondestructive way. It replaces any feeling of isolation that
the individual may have had, and it fosters identification
with others. Group members experience permissiveness,
tolerance, emotional support, and strength of ego through a
sense of belonging. Of all the mechanisms listed,
Acceptance has the most to do with the social climate and
was statistically the most frequent concept utilized in the
study.

The group leader sets a social climate of acceptance
by behaving in a permissive manner void of value
judgments. The group will tend to test the limits of the
leader's permissiveness (acting-out behavior), and the
leader must be able to demonstrate the genuineness of his
or her acceptance, bearing in mind the distinction between
accepting the individual, but not necessarily accepting his
or her past or present behavior.

Ventilation

This is one of the basic mechanisms of group work because it refers to the expression of a member's true feelings--the unloading of things that have been bothering him or her. In many ways, it is a verbal acting out. However, in the experiential group situation the attempt is to get the group members not only to express their negative or hostile feelings but also to examine them. This would apply equally to feelings of guilt or anxiety and the fantasy material which might stimulate these.

It is generally felt that once group members have expressed their feelings, they are in a better position, emotionally, to deal with their conflicts that often keep them from gaining personal insights or making behavioral changes.

Reality Testing

As pointed out earlier, the group offers the opportunity for testing a group member's defenses or mode of operation through the feedback they get from other group members. "Working through" is the term generally used to describe this. Perhaps Reality Testing is one of the most difficult and uncomfortable aspects of group experience for the individual member, not only because it necessarily involves change, but because it is necessarily critical. The main reason Reality Testing is most effective in the group situation is that reactions and feedback are coming from peers rather than from an authority figure. This is without a doubt one of the most important components in making the group experience work. It demonstrates the power that feedback plays in creating personal insight.

Transference

Transference is the displacement of emotional feelings more appropriate to significant individuals in a member's early life (usually the father and mother) to individuals one meets in his or her day-to-day encounters. In the group situation, this would apply to the leader and other group members.

There is some question about the degree of transference that takes place in a experiential group situation. However, it is generally agreed that it does set up an accepting climate because close relationships are formed and recognized, and, this in turn, facilitates the reality testing process. The group leader, however, should stay alert and aware of his or her own feelings to the group members in order to avoid countertransference.

Intellectualization

In the group process, the group members learn new ways of handling situations and of reacting to their environment and those in it. Hopefully, they gain better self-understanding, an ability to analyze some of their own feelings, and give up some of their past ineffectual responses. This type of insight is often the first step toward behavioral change.

In dealing with this mechanism, group leaders must avoid overintellectualization and falling into the role of lecturers; they must be careful that the group does not become a philosophical one instead of one using

Intellectualization as an escape from anxiety producing feelings with the possibility of behavioral change.

Interaction

This term is quite self-explanatory and refers to the inter- and cross-action of the group. It is generally felt that most group interaction has the potential for behavioral change and perhaps depends most upon the leader's ability to handle it. The primary role of the group leader is to conduct the Interaction and keep it productive.

Universalization

Basically, this is the idea that as a group member you are not alone, and that other group members are experiencing similar problems such as feelings of guilt, fear, frustration, etc. Group members who are struggling with what they consider an overwhelming problem find that it is not unique and other group members have been through a similar situation, perhaps even more intense.

The role of the group leader here is to emphasize the similarities in life experiences of group members. By doing so, the group leader creates one of the strongest group bonding experiences of the entire group process. In the experiential group experience, Universalization and the fact that others have shared similar experiences can produce some dramatic personal effects.

Altruism

Altruism is the concern for others, as opposed to a selfish concern. In the group, it implies self-sacrifice in the interest and benefit of other group members. It is closely related to Acceptance but implies more. Perhaps its greatest effect comes from the feeling a person gets from having been effective in helping another individual. The helping group member takes over the role of group leader during this exchange. The group member receiving the help seems to accept Reality Testing and/or other help from a peer than he or she would from the group leader.

The effectiveness of the group leader lies in his or her willingness to allow the group members to play the role of group leader. The only danger here is that there are often individuals in the group who will quickly jump into this role in order to escape any examination of their own behavior or to avoid facing the possible attack from others.

Spectator Learning

In speaking of the mechanism of Spectator Learning, the passive participant is referred to as the silent member who only learns by listening and observing the group process. The role of group leader is to allay personal anxiety about the "nonparticipating" member because the group itself usually becomes active in bringing out the silent member. Nonparticipation should not be fostered in groups or excused on the grounds of Spectator Learning. Needless to say, if all group members became silent, there would be a questionable group experience.

Chapter 5

PHASES OF THE EXPERIENTIAL GROUP DEVELOPMENT

Experiential groups appear to move through definite developmental stages at different rates of speed, depending upon several factors such as the composition of the group and the group leader's style. Groups have the tendency to move regularly from preoccupation with authority to preoccupation with personal relations.

Bennis and Shephard (1956) found that group members who find comfort in rules of procedure, an agenda, an expert, etc., are referred to as "dependent." Members who are discomforted by authoritative structure are called "counterdependent." Members who cannot rest until they have stabilized a relatively high degree of intimacy with all other group members are called "overpersonal." Members who tend to avoid intimacy with any of the others are called "counterpersonal." Thus, in the group's movement from preoccupation with authority relations to preoccupation with personal relations, these "dependent and personal" aspects of member personality become clearly defined.

Mintz (1967) postulates that the various phases (on a different level) through which groups seem to move are namely: (1) the anxiety phase, (2) the hostility phase, (3) the dependency phase, and (4) the appreciation phase.

Thelen and Dickerman (1949) also define four phases through which a group must pass in its growth towards the ability to operate efficiently. In the first phase, various members of the group quickly attempt to establish their customary places in the leadership hierarchy. Next comes a period of frustration and conflict brought about by the group leader's steadfast rejection of the concept of "peck order" and the authoritarian atmosphere in which the concept of "peck order" is rooted. The third phase sees the development of cohesiveness among members of the group, accompanied by a certain amount of complacency and smugness. This third phase seems to be characterized by determination to achieve and maintain harmony at all costs. This phase is unstable because it is unrealistic, and thus it gives way to a fourth phase. In this fourth phase, the members retain the group centeredness and sensitivities which characterize the third phase, but they develop also a sense of purpose and urgency which make the group potentially an effective social instrument for insight and possible behavioral change.

Bion (1963) thinks of a group in terms of a series of emotional states or basic assumption cultures in which the affective need of the group is associated with the work the group is trying to accomplish. The basic assumption culture pertains to the situation in the group as a whole. By the term "basic assumption" Bion is referring to an implicit need which is shared by various members of the group; that is to say, the group acts "as if" it shares this certain need.

Bion has postulated that there are three distinct emotional states or basic assumption cultures found in groups: Pairing--counterpairing (moving toward intimacy or isolation); Dependency--counterdependency (reliance on or rejection of external authority); Fight--flight (fighting or fleeing from stress). In addition to these emotional cultures, a fourth, a work culture exists. It is Bion's belief that the work activity of any group is always influenced to some extent by the emotional states of concern. These emotional states are nonpurposeful, instinctual, and not under conscious control. The emotional cultures require no learning or special training, but arise from the impulsive expression of needs. Participation in the work culture, however, is learned and demands a certain commitment and sophistication on the part of a group and skill on the part of the group leader.

In the group situation, one finds that group members seem to have a preference for certain work-emotional cultures over others. These preferences are expressed in behavior and sometimes directly through statements such as, "I prefer the group when we deal with our own problems rather than being given a group agenda." This would, of course, be work in the dependency culture; the basic assumption being that the group is acting as if it can function on its own.

The work culture always occurs in combinations with one of the emotional cultures, and the emotional culture frequently is a changing thing. In any given group situation, it will be found that the emotional culture shifts and the relationship between work and emotionality may change several times in terms of dominance.

Bion (1965) speaks of two feeling aspects (security and anxiety) as accounting for the establishment of the culture found and its eventful dissolution. The emotional culture meets the need for a rather immediate satisfaction, such as a need to speak out or to express a primitive drive. The work culture satisfies the need to be a responsible member of the group and to be rewarded through the feeling of having helped others. The dominance of work verses emotionality is best understood when the needs of each member are met analyzed. The ideal combination is one in which work and emotional cultures are intertwined so that needs are met in such a way that neither frustration nor anxiety is produced. In its development, a group can be seen as going through successive phases in which one work-emotional culture gives way to another. Anxiety and need gratification determine the shift from one culture to another and the dominance of a work culture over the emotional culture.

Martin and Hill (1957) suggest that groups go through a developmental process which they have divided into six discreet phases. Each phase is described in terms of the major problem confronting the group and the characteristic behaviors to be found at that phase level. In addition, there are transitional stages between these developmental plateaus, and it is at these transitional stages that potential for movement to the next phase level occurs. They feel that groups have distinct and common growth patterns which are discernable, observable, and predictable. Phases and their transitional periods can be thought of as points along the continuum, and thus the theory can be demonstrated in a developmental scale as follows:

Scale of Group Development

PHASES	TITLE OF PHASE
Phase I	Individual Unshared Behavior in an Imposed Structure

Transition from I to II

Phase II	Reactivation of Fixated Interpersonal Attitudes

Transition from II to III

Phase III	Exploration of Interpersonal Potential Within the Group

Transition from III to IV

Phase IV	Awareness of Interrelationships, Sub-groupings and Power Structures

Transition from IV to V

Phase V	Consciousness of Group Dynamics and Group Process Problems

Transition from V to VI

Phase VI	The Group as an Effective Integrative Creative-Social Instrument

Phase I: At this developmental level, identification with the group is minimal, with the social isolation of group members being most characteristic. The group behavior is stimulated by past experience, with the group being essentially a collection of parts held together in loose association by a vague awareness of the leader's role. The role of the leader in this phase is to give structure to the group and providing a focal point around which the members can revolve.

In the transitional period from Phase I to Phase II, the leadership role begins to emerge more realistically for the group members and becomes generally acknowledged. In addition, the group members are beginning to become more aware of others in the group, and the beginning phase of the experiential group experience is beginning to develop.

Phase II: Group members are now being reacted to as individuals, but the reactions are in terms of learned personality stereotypes. In other words, the reactions are manifestations of the transference phenomena; they are "ghosts" of earlier interpersonal experiences, with little recognition of the individuality of the personalities present. The group leader is also reacted to in a stereotypical fashion. The most positive aspect of this phase is the fact that there is a growing awareness of individuals, and socialization is taking place.

In the transitional period from Phase II to Phase III, the operating on social stereotypes is beginning to break down, and the reality of the individual members begins to emerge. The group leader's role can be helpful in getting the group members to see the discrepancies that exist between their stereotyping of the group leader and other group members.   The importance is being able to see people as they really are.

Phase III: The group now begins to adopt the spirit of "active emotional exchange" and there is much time spent in the exploration of the individual in the group. Membership is valued at this point, and absences or any disruption of the group composition is viewed with considerable concern. The group leader's role becomes less active, other than to support, encourage, and attempt to bring forth the creative abilities of the individual group members.

In the transition period between Phase III and Phase IV, boredom tends to set in, and the feeling of merely going through motions and lack of forward movement becomes prevalent. The group leader makes the group aware of its dissatisfaction and helps the group move into an exploration of the relationships within the group.

Phase IV: The group now moves from a recognition of individual personalities to an exploration and an awareness of the relationships that have developed in terms of sub-grouping and power structures. The role of the leader is to assist the group in exploring these relationships, mostly by pointing them out. The leadership now becomes a shifting thing, with individuals in the group periodically assuming the leadership role and rivalries developing. The leader remains external to this power struggle and can be helpful by pointing out the sub-grouping, the supporters, the effects that an emotionally needy member has on the group, and the power struggle that is going on.

The transition period from Phase IV to Phase V is again marked by dissatisfaction, but this time it stems from the sub-groupings, the rivalries, and the tension state produced by this operational level. The group leader assists the group by pointing out its dissatisfaction, the factionalism that exists, and provides the group with some model or concept for moving ahead to higher levels of work.

Phase V: It is here that the group begins to sense itself as a functioning group and may begin to be concerned with learning and applying concepts of how particular group functions are being helpful to individual group members. The group can sustain this high level of work for only short periods before reverting to lower levels of operation. The group leader now has many demands in terms of skill, while assisting the group in investigating and understanding the implications that the group has for its individual members.

In the transition period from Phase V to Phase VI, the group, which has now been able to describe and diagnose its own process, feels the need to remedy the undesirable features which have been uncovered. The group leader assists the group members in making them conscious of their struggle and supports them in their belief that group problem solving (insight) and behavioral change can take place.

Phase VI: Very few groups ever actually reach this stage of development and, in fact, seldom would ever find it necessary. To quote Martin and Hill, "To operate at this level with any degree of consistency probably carries with it the assumption that the members are more effective and mentally healthier than the national average." The group can now do cooperative problem solving, diagnose its own process problems, and develop techniques to handle these. The group leader almost fades into the membership, and this is because the members have become themselves capable leaders. The only differentiation the leader may have is the experience and training, and thus the group leader has made the transition to a group resource person--a member of the group.

Chapter 6

ROLE OF THE GROUP LEADER

Many years before the study of human behavior was formalized, the importance of the communicator in influencing people was recognized. Hovland and others (1953) found that if the communicator had a striking or charismatic personality, the message was more likely to be accepted. Most group theorists are in agreement that the role of the group leader is to assist group members to achieve one or more of the following objectives:

1. increased insight and awareness,
2. increased insight into interpersonal relations and one's own competence in them,
3. skill practice in improving interpersonal competence,
4. increased understanding of the nature, dynamics, and working of groups,

5. insight and/or skill practice in problem solving, and
6. insight and practice in better functioning in an organizational system.

It is difficult to explore the meaning of communication if group leaders are not reasonably aware of the "quirks" in their own makeup which tend to block out hearing the responses of the group. This brings to the conscious level certain unacceptable things in their personalities, thus critically curtailing their ability to reflect, empathize, and interpret. Johnson (1963) writes that the group leaders must be willing to examine their emotional impact in a group of people and be able to recognize that their own conscious and unconscious mechanisms can markedly influence the behavior of a group of people.

Foulkes (1949) suggested that the term "conductor" be used to designate the role of a group leader. The group leader encourages passive people to be more actively expressive and encourages active people to be more passively expressive. As a conductor the expression of each person's character in the group is brought out, just as an orchestra leader brings out the appropriate instrumental voicings in an orchestra.

The outcome of any growth/change that occurs in an experiential group is highly dependent on the special abilities of the group leader. Anyone can talk about emotional growth, feeling, trusting, awareness, freedom, and self-fulfillment, but without some very specific training (e.g., M.D. psychiatrist, M.A. or Ph.D. psychologist, M.S.W. social worker, and M.S. or Ph.D. in organizational development or human resources) as to the psychological importance of these concepts, the growth/change impact of the group experience must be questioned. Most group specialists agree that group dynamics can create intense emotional and intellectual reactions, and what is needed is well-trained people who can deal with problems (and successes) before, while, and after they happen.

Chapter 7

GUIDELINES FOR CONDUCTING THE EXPERIENTIAL GROUP

Everett Shostrom (1977), in his book <u>Actualizing Therapy</u>, suggests that group leaders use the American Psychological Association (APA) guidelines in conducting the small group experiences. Many of his suggestions are very appropriate for use as guidelines for conducting the experiential group. The following information is considered to be of paramount importance:

1. an explicit statement of the goals and purpose of the group experience,
2. types and styles of group dynamic exercises/techniques to be employed,
3. the educational background and training of the group leader(s),

4. the professional and ethical obligations of the group leader and group members,
5. the contracted understanding of the purpose and direction of the experiential group,
6. the relationship between the group experience and the evaluative group analysis of the group process itself, and
7. issues of confidentiality and its relationship to overall group development.

The guidelines for the experiential group process differs somewhat from the more traditional psychotherapy groups. Again the emphasis is on the "here and now" without the examination of deep, unresolved interpersonal conflicts. Group members, especially students of a group dynamics class, are looking to learn the workings academically of the group process. The goals are again restated as insight driven into ideas, concepts, and theories, and in some cases, possible cognitive/behavioral changes. The group sessions themselves include some lecturing/discussion by the group leader on theory issues, various research techniques for establishing the phase development process, suggested books, journals, and articles are included for continued enhancement of the role of the experiential group.

Chapter 8

EXPERIENTIAL GROUP ACTIVITIES AND EXERCISES

Activities and exercises are needed in the beginning of the experiential group to establish personal awareness, group interactions, conceptualization of interpersonal relationships, and increased self-knowledge and sensitivity toward others. From the very beginning, the group leader's role is to work toward shifting responsibility for structuring, understanding, and controlling the group activities to the group members themselves. One of the major keys is to establish the ability for group members to understand the importance of feedback from other group members and the role it can play in improving communication skills. Often with the proper introductory structural exercises and activities, group members learn how to disclose feelings, gain conflict-reduction skills, and find enjoyment from working in the experiential group process.

I offer the following for possible consideration while at the same time maintaining flexibility for group leaders to express their own preferences in the selection process.

MEMORY EXERCISE FOR THE FIRST SESSION

Purpose:

To develop the personal connection to the experiential group.

Method:

As soon as the first group session begins, ask the group members to rearrange the seating so as to make one large circle. Then starting from the left or right (whichever you may prefer) ask the first group member to state his or her first name. Before the second member can say his or her name, ask him or her to repeat the first name and then add his or her name. This is usually the icebreaker because the rest of the group members quickly realize what is expected of them. So, the next member must repeat the two previous names and then add his or her name, and so it goes all the way around the circle.

If you start from the left, the "groans" will come from the right and vice-versa. After a while, you will find them alert and focused while waiting their turn to recall the names. If a group member needs help in the recall process, it should always be offered. Complimenting members with excellent memory skills also motivates the other members to do their best.

Once you have gone around the circle, then you reverse the process, which balances out the exercise for both sides of the circle. You should also practice the names because, in the end, the group members will challenge you to perform the same task.

This simple name recall exercise could be one of the most important 30 minutes in getting your experiential group off the ground.

INTRODUCTION OF GROUP MEMBERS

Purpose:

    To get each group member involved; to model self-disclosure; to provide opportunity for modeling interview techniques.

Method:

    Each group member is to introduce themselves to the group. The introduction should include something that would not ordinarily be said by the group member when first meeting a stranger. The group leader should begin self-introduction. Topics of effective self-disclosure include:

- work/career objectives,
- political issues,
- hobbies,
- personal experiences, and
- educational goals.

Alternate Method:

    Pair off group members--allow 5 or 10 minutes for them to get acquainted and then have them introduce each other to the group including their personal reactions to each other.

Alternate Activity:

    Have each group member reveal his or her thoughts while on the way to the group session.

GROUP LEADER ANALYSIS

First Impression Perception Checking:

What kind of person is the group leader? In answering this question, you may wish to consider some or all of the following characteristics or elements, along with others which you think are important or evident:

1. ethnic background,
2. geographic background,
3. educational background,
4. age,
5. religious background,
6. general belief system, values, etc.,
7. family status (marital status, children, etc.),
8. hobbies/leisure time activities,
9. work/occupational experiences/employment background,
10. health/physical condition,
11. temperament (permissive or directive verbal or physical, active or inactive, emotional or cool, leader or follower, etc.),
12. skills/abilities,
13. dress/grooming,
14. strong likes/dislikes, and
15. other impressions not covered above.

LIFE VALUES

<u>Purpose</u>:
Self Awareness; awareness of individual differences about life values; and disclosure.

<u>Method</u>:
1) Lecture about individual values (can include value formation) and potential conflict resulting from life values;
2) Complete Life Value Inventory;   3.) Small group discussion (taking turns) in context of:
   a) What was new to me? (something of which I was unaware) (Test feedback).
   b) Do I agree/disagree with feedback? (Why?)
   c) How can I use the feedback?

Instructions for Life Value Inventory:

1. There are 100 statements on this inventory.
2. You are to read each statement carefully.
3. If a statement is DEFINITLEY TRUE for you, circle the number 10 following that statement.
4. If a statement is MOSTLY TRUE for you, circle the number 7 following that statement.
5. If you are UNDECIDED about a statement, circle the number 5 following that statement.
6. If a statement is MOSTLY FALSE for you, circle the number 3 following that statement.
7. If a statement is DEFINITELY FALSE for you, circle the 0 following that statement.

If you change your mind, feel free to change your answer(s).

1. I have a regular physical check-up by my doctor every year.	10	7	5	3	0
2. I often attend church on a regular basis.	10	7	5	3	0
3. I enjoy attending musical concerts.	10	7	5	3	0
4. It is important that I have developed friendships.	10	7	5	3	0
5. I donate to charities that I feel are worthwhile.	10	7	5	3	0
6. I envy the way movie stars are recognized wherever they go.	10	7	5	3	0
7. I would like to have enough money to retire by the time I am 50.	10	7	5	3	0
8. I would rather spend an evening at home with my family than out with my friends.	10	7	5	3	0
9. I enjoy making decisions which involve other people.	10	7	5	3	0

10.If I had the musical talent, I would like to be a song writer or singer.	10	7	5	3	0
11.I have a close relationship with either my mother or my father.	10	7	5	3	0
12.I have taught a Sunday school class or otherwise taken an active part in my church.	10	7	5	3	0
13.I am willing to spend time helping another student who is having difficulty with his or her studies.	10	7	5	3	0
14.Even at the same salary, I would rather be the boss than just another employee.	10	7	5	3	0
15.I have a special appreciation for beautiful things.	10	7	5	3	0
16.If I had the talent, I would like to appear regularly on television.	10	7	5	3	0
17.I would like to counsel and advise people and help them with their psychological problems.	10	7	5	3	0

18.I would enjoy associating with movie stars and other celebrities.	10	7	5	3	0
19.I have a regular dental check-up at least once a year.	10	7	5	3	0
20.I enjoy writing short stories.	10	7	5	3	0
21.I would rather spend a summer working to earn money than go on vacation.	10	7	5	3	0
22.I like to attend parties.	10	7	5	3	0
23.I think it would be fun to write a screen play for television.	10	7	5	3	0
24.I believe in a God who answers prayers.	10	7	5	3	0
25.I prefer being an executive than just a mid-level manager.	10	7	5	3	0
26.I would spend my last $500 for needed dental work rather than for a week's vacation at my favorite resort.	10	7	5	3	0
27.I enjoy giving presents to members of my family.	10	7	5	3	0

28. If I were a professor, I would rather teach creative writing than business law.	10	7	5	3	0
29. I often daydream about things that I would like to have if I could make enough money to buy them.	10	7	5	3	0
30. I enjoy giving parties.	10	7	5	3	0
31. I am willing to write letters for people in nursing homes.	10	7	5	3	0
32. It would be very satisfying to act in movies or television.	10	7	5	3	0
33. When I am ill, I usually see or call a doctor.	10	7	5	3	0
34. I believe that tithing (giving 1/10 of one's earnings to the church) is one's duty to God.	10	7	5	3	0
35. I enjoy taking part in the discussion at the family dinner table.	10	7	5	3	0
36. I enjoy visiting art museums.	10	7	5	3	0
37. I like to write poetry.	10	7	5	3	0

38.I like to be around people most of the time.	10	7	5	3	0
39.When with a friend, I like to be the one who decides what we will do or where we will go.	10	7	5	3	0
40.Someday, I would like to live in a large expensive home.	10	7	5	3	0
41.I pray to God about my problems.	10	7	5	3	0
42.If I knew a family that had no food for Christmas dinner, I would try to provide it.	10	7	5	3	0
43.I like to spend holidays with my family.	10	7	5	3	0
44.I like to see my name in print (newspaper).	10	7	5	3	0
45.I would rather take a course in freehand drawing than a class in mathematics.	10	7	5	3	0
46.I do not like to spend an entire evening alone.	10	7	5	3	0
47.If the salary were the same, I would rather be a financial analyst than a college professor.	10	7	5	3	0

48.I have expensive tastes.	10	7	5	3	0
49.I can tell the difference between a really fine painting or drawing and an ordinary one.	10	7	5	3	0
50.If I had regular headaches, I would consult a doctor even if aspirin seemed to lessen the pain.	10	7	5	3	0
51.I have several very close friends.	10	7	5	3	0
52.I expect to provide music lessons for my children.	10	7	5	3	0
53.It is important that grace be said before meals.	10	7	5	3	0
54.I sometimes miss sleep to stay up late with friends.	10	7	5	3	0
55.I usually get at least 8 hours of sleep each night.	10	7	5	3	0
56.I like to design things.	10	7	5	3	0
57.I would like to be respected for my accomplishments.	10	7	5	3	0
58.I would like to feel a sense of satisfaction from nursing a sick person back to health.	10	7	5	3	0

59. I care what my parents think about the things I do.	10	7	5	3	0
60. I daydream about making a lot of money.	10	7	5	3	0
61. I like to be the chairperson at meetings.	10	7	5	3	0
62. It is thrilling to come up with an original idea and put it to use.	10	7	5	3	0
63. I believe that there is life after death.	10	7	5	3	0
64. I would welcome a person of another race as a neighbor.	10	7	5	3	0
65. If I were in the television field, I would rather be an actor than a script writer.	10	7	5	3	0
66. I enjoy decorating my room at home.	10	7	5	3	0
67. I enjoy a picnic with my family.	10	7	5	3	0
68. As an adult, I want to earn a much higher salary than the average worker.	10	7	5	3	0
69. I am careful to eat a balanced diet each day.	10	7	5	3	0

70. I often influence other students concerning the classes in which they enroll.	10	7	5	3	0
71. I would like to be written up in Who's Who.	10	7	5	3	0
72. I read the Bible or other religious writings regularly.	10	7	5	3	0
73. If I were in the clothing industry, I would enjoy creating new styles.	10	7	5	3	0
74. I look forward to an evening out with a group of friends.	10	7	5	3	0
75. When I am with a group of people I like to be the one "in charge."	10	7	5	3	0
76. I dislike being financially dependent on others.	10	7	5	3	0
77. When a friend is in trouble, I feel I must offer comfort.	10	7	5	3	0
78. I love my parents.	10	7	5	3	0
79. I never skip meals.	10	7	5	3	0
80. I have a collection of CD's.	10	7	5	3	0

81.I have a particular friend with whom I can discuss my interpersonal thoughts.	10	7	5	3	0
82.I believe that God created man in his own image.	10	7	5	3	0
83.I enjoy buying special things for members of my family.	10	7	5	3	0
84.I enjoy having people recognize me wherever I am.	10	7	5	3	0
85.I like planning activities for other people.	10	7	5	3	0
86.I do not smoke.	10	7	5	3	0
87.I get a good feeling when I do things that help others.	10	7	5	3	0
88.Someday, I would like to write a novel.	10	7	5	3	0
89.I would put up with undesirable living conditions in order to work at a job that paid extremely well.	10	7	5	3	0
90.I belong to several clubs and organizations.	10	7	5	3	0

91. If I ask God for forgiveness, my sins are forgiven.	10	7	5	3	0
92. I would enjoy having my picture in the school yearbook more than it has been in the past.	10	7	5	3	0
93. I often organize group activities.	10	7	5	3	0
94. When I see a newly-constructed building, I consider beauty and architectural style as much as its practical use.	10	7	5	3	0
95. I respect my mother and father.	10	7	5	3	0
96. I like to design or make things that have not been made before.	10	7	5	3	0
97. Some of the hobbies that I would like to engage in are quite expensive.	10	7	5	3	0
98. I enjoy classical music.	10	7	5	3	0
99. I would never use potentially harmful drugs because of what they may do to my body.	10	7	5	3	0
100. I am kind to animals.	10	7	5	3	0

Life Value Inventory Summary Sheet:

Fame	Money	Power	Religion	Humanism
6.___	7.___	9.___	2.___	5.___
16.___	21.___	14.___	12.___	13.___
18.___	29.___	25.___	24.___	17.___
32.___	40.___	39.___	34.___	31.___
44.___	48.___	47.___	41.___	42.___
57.___	60.___	61.___	53.___	58.___
65.___	68.___	70.___	63.___	64.___
71.___	76.___	75.___	72.___	77.___
84.___	89.___	85.___	82.___	87.___
92.___	97.___	93.___	91.___	100.___
T___	T___	T___	T___	T___

Family	Health	Aesthetic	Creative	Social
8.___	1.___	3.___	10.___	4.___
11.___	19.___	15.___	20.___	22.___
27.___	26.___	28.___	23.___	30.___
35.___	33.___	36.___	37.___	38.___
43.___	50.___	49.___	45.___	46.___
59.___	55.___	52.___	56.___	51.___
67.___	69.___	66.___	62.___	54.___
78.___	79.___	80.___	73.___	74.___
83.___	86.___	94.___	88.___	81.___
95.___	99.___	98.___	96.___	90.___
T___	T___	T___	T___	T___

BODY DRAWING

Purpose:
1. To introduce concepts of body language in non-verbal communication.
2. To increase participants awareness of their own body messages.

Method:
1. Have each group member draw a picture of his or her body. Point out that artistic ability is not important and that the drawing should not take more than 10-15 minutes to do.
2. Have group members assume the position of the drawing.
3. As group members remain in these positions, the group leader slowly asks the following questions:
   a. What or who are you?
   b. What role are you?
   c. What have you created?
   d. What image do you project to the world?
   e. Where are you most conscious of yourself?
   f. What kind of life experience do you hope to get from this stance?
   g. How does this image interfere with relationships?
   h. How does this image interfere with communication?
   i. How does this image inhibit aliveness-excitement?

4. Group members are then asked to share some of their answers.

This can be done in large or small groups. Questions can be distributed on paper or reread by the group leader so that group members can write down answers.

CAR-ANIMAL-FOOD

<u>Purpose</u>:
To structure direct feedback in a light and relatively harmless way.

<u>Method</u>:
1. Group members form sub-groups of 5 or 6.
2. One person is selected for beginning.
3. The group member to the left, and each other subsequently in turn, tells the first person, "If you were a car, you would be a _____."
4. After all have labeled the first person, they go around the circle and tell why they labeled as they did; i.e., "You are a BMW because _____."
5. Each group member takes his or her turn receiving feedback.
6. At this point, or at the end of the exercise, or both, the entire group discusses the experience.
7. Within the same subgroups, the same thing is repeated but changed to, "If you were an animal, you would be a _____." and "If you were a food, you would be a _____."

FEEDBACK QUESTIONS

Purpose:

    To structure feedback between group members (note: particularly useful midway through or even on the last day).

Method:
1. Instruct group members to answer the following questions:

From among the group members, whom would you choose:

-- for a supervisor?

-- to send on an important and dangerous mission?

-- as a friend for recreation?

-- to seek help from if you were in serious trouble?

-- to discuss a new idea with?

-- to escort your wife/girlfriend across the country?

2. Have all group members circulate and give some feedback to every other participant, making it a point to tell them if they were chosen as the answer to one of the questions and why they were chosen.

3. Optional--tally the responses to the questions and analyze why some were popular responses to certain questions.

ACCEPTANCE – REJECTION EXERCISE

Purpose:

To demonstrate how it feels to be rejected; and the importance of acceptance.

Method:

From small groups of five or six, select two members to leave the room.

Those leaving the room (leavers) are told that those remaining in the room (remainers) will be given a topic to discuss and that the leavers are to do the following:

1. return to their original groups;
2. determine as quickly as possible what the topic is; and
3. participate in the discussion as constructively as possible.

Remainers are given a topic for discussion and are told to identify one leaver to be "accepted" and one to be "rejected." Upon their return, the "accepted" leaver's ideas will be sought and valued while the "rejected" leaver's ideas will be neither sought or valued.

After they return to their groups and a brief discussion period ensues, the leavers are asked to share their reactions to the experience with the entire group. All group members are then encouraged to discuss the experience sharing their own reactions and feelings.

COMPETING FOR ATTENTION

Purpose:
    To demonstrate techniques for monopolizing attention (volume, topic, questions, and contact).

Method:
1. Participants are divided into groups of three.
2. One person is designated the object of attention and sits between the other two.
3. The other two people compete with each other for the focused-person's attention.
4. Participants rotate and repeat the experience until each has been the object.

Note: It is possible to do this in groups of four.

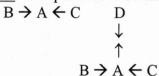

MICRO – LAB

Purpose:

To promote individual involvement; to structure experience of looking at oneself in relation to the group experience; to demonstrate self-disclosure; and to contrast with communication.

Method:

1. Each group member pairs with another with whom he or she is not already well acquainted.
2. The pairs take 2 or 3 minutes to become acquainted.
3. Pairs then move together to form groups of four—then two groups of four make a group of eight.
4. One member of each pair moves to the center forming an inner group of four, with other members forming an outer group of observers.
5. Those in inner group take about five minutes to get acquainted. (Group leader note: the result is usually topic-controlled conversation – business, sports, opinions – generally shallow emotional content. Frequently one person will dominate the interaction.)
6. Original pairs then discuss what happened to help or hinder the group in getting acquainted.
7. Outer group now moves to center and gets acquainted by sharing something personal about themselves (peak experiences, attitudes, etc.)
8. Discuss with entire group what happened. Contrast first and second inner-group experiences.

9. Reform into groups of eight.
10. Get acquainted further, but non-verbally (5 minutes).

MICRO – LAB II

Alternative Method:
1. Non-Verbal Exercise:
   a. Circulate around and pick out someone with whom you would like to become better acquainted.
   b. Thumb wrestle (demonstrate).
   c. Hands together free motion; take turns as leader;   no   designated   leader (demonstrate).
2. Groups of two combine into groups of four for discussion of what you learned about self and partner and other reactions to experience.
   a. Start discussion by introducing your partner in terms of what you learned from the exercises.
   b. Each group member describes what he or she learned about from the exercise and reacts to partner's introduction.
   c. General discussion of reactions, if any.

SHOW-N-TELL

Purpose:

To provide practice in self-disclosure at increasingly personal levels.

Method:

At various times during the group process, divide the members into groups of 4 or 5 and instruct them to share.

1. Ask them to say something about themselves that they wouldn't ordinarily say in such a circumstance; e.g., single word description, favorite food or activity, what they do when they don't have to do anything?
2. Describe your most difficult experience with each of the following:
    a. Physical
    b. Intellectual
    c. Emotional
3. Describe your most emotional experience (not necessarily difficult, can be positive or negative).
4. Tell of your closest call to dying and/or tell how you handled the death of another person.
5. Describe your most positive experience.
6. Share the biggest problem you are now facing or one you have recently resolved, and how.

POSITIVE FEEDBACK

Purpose:
<u>Purpose</u>:
To bring awareness to the tendency to focus on only the negative and to enhance self-esteem

<u>Method</u>:
Select one group member at a time for positive feedback. Have each group member make positive comments based on group observation about the group member receiving the positive feedback. Based on the size of the group, each member of the group will receive considerable positive feedback, some of which will be duplicated by other group members. The duplication only reinforces the positive effect on the receiving group member.

This is an excellent exercise after there has been enough imposed group structure to the group to form individual personalities that other group members can identify. Usually this will occur after three or four group sessions. It can be useful when the group leader notices that group members are suffering from self-esteem issues and could use an uplifting session.

IDEAL SELF

Purpose:
    To help create the concept that it is important to have a sense of direction and forward movement in one's life.

Method:
    Give the group members a 15-minute break to conceptualize how they would present their ideal self to the group. (For example, future goals, aspirations, lifestyle preferences, appearance, overcoming obstacles, career plans, etc.) Then have each member present his or her ideal self to the group.
    This is an exercise that emphasizes the role of experiential groups offering the opportunity for reality testing in a very non-threatening manner.

Alternative Method:
    This exercise can also be acted out by having each group member do the following:
1. Stand up with feet planted without any forward or backward movement and him or her discuss life's implications of such a rigid stance.
2. Walk backward and have him or her discuss life's implications of walking in reverse.
3. Walk forward and have him or her discuss life's implications of walking in reverse.

SELF-DISCLOSURE EXERCISE FOR THE ADVANCED SESSIONS

Purpose:

Serves as an excellent exercise for Reality Testing, and as an evaluation of the ability to give and receive feedback.

Method:

Break the group into small sub-groups (4-6 members). It is important that they are isolated in a private area where there is total privacy, with minimal chance of interruption. The following instructions should be given by the group leader to each sub-group:

1. Take a few minutes and reflect on how you would present your own perception of self to the group.
2. Have one group member start by presenting self-perception to the group for approximately 5 minutes.
3. Once the group member is finished, start on the right or left and have each group member give feedback as to his or her perception of that group member.
4. Remember the rule that only one person talks at a time.
5. There is to be no response to the feedback from group members whether it is positive or negative.
6. Continuing on the right or left have the next group member give his or her perception of him or herself for 5 minutes.

7. Again once completed, that group member will receive feedback from each group member.
8. The group has completed the task when all the group members have gone through the perception check (Reality Testing).
9. Allow 30 minutes for an open discussion about some of the thoughts and feelings the exercise provoked.

EMPATHETIC SKILL TRAINING

Purpose:

To help group members understand the importance of putting oneself into the other person's shoes, and entering the other person's world.

Method:

Empathetic training skills (developing active listeners) can be used throughout the group sessions. It can work very well when there is a member-centered focus. If a member needs to talk, then it is often an excellent time for the group leader to introduce the basics for empathetic training. They would include the following:

1. listen for the main idea,
2. give feedback,
3. listen for feelings as well as facts, and
4. paraphrase .

The group leader can continually discuss the importance of empathy throughout the sessions. Empathy scales can be developed by rating the group members (e.g. 1 through 10) on their ability to develop empathy skills.

In summary, many people think of experiential group dynamics as a collection of activities. One must be reminded that group dynamics as a whole is the study of the behavior in groups. Activities used in the proper context can be very beneficial in establishing a strong working experiential group process. Structure in the beginning is necessary because the group members will more than likely be feeling a fairly high degree of anxiety. The general objective is to increase the interactional relationships between group members whereby at the end of the process the group can begin to feel a shared reality, personally as well as professionally. Planned activities can provide a safe beginning to build on as group members develop a comfort that eventually will allow them to listen, question, ask, and explore feelings and ideas that they would probably disguise or ignore. The interactional group process can help the group members learn about their own motivation or lack of it, the social and personal obstacles to their goals and aspirations, and the contribution that a group dynamics experience can contribute to self-determination.

Chapter 9

SUPPORTIVE THEORY FOR THE EXPERIENTIAL GROUP

Since the development phase model is often emphasized as the main directional goal for the experiential group, then it would seem appropriate to introduce developmental theory soon after the introductory group session. Developmental psychologists who study physical, mental, and social/personal change throughout the human life cycle have added considerably to the understanding as to how human behavior can possibly progress through a fixed period series of steps. Research can cast some doubt on whether life proceeds through neatly defined, age-linked stages. Nevertheless for the experiential group experience, these stages of development can be very useful.

Erik Erikson (1963) felt that when it came to understanding life, experiential learning was the only worthwhile kind. He felt that each stage of development that included trust versus mistrust, identity versus role confusion, and generativity versus stagnation, reflected a conflict involving personal and social demands. The eight stage process developed by Erikson is as follows:

APPROXIMATE AGE	I. PSYCHO/SOCIAL CONFLICT
Stage 1--Infancy (0-2)	Trust vs. Mistrust If needs are met, infant develops a sense of basic trust.
Stage 2--Childhood (2-3)	Autonomy vs. shame and doubt Children learn independence and self-confidence through personal and social exploration.
Stage 3--Play Age (3-5)	Initiative vs. Guilt Children learn through the role of trial and error how to develop the beginning of self-control.
Stage 4--School Age (6-12)	Competence vs. Inferiority Children learn to feel effective (skill development) or inadequate.
Stage 5 -- Adolescence (13-20)	Identity vs. role confusion Role testing by adolescents leads to an acceptable identity.

Stage 6--Young Adulthood (20-40)	Intimacy vs. isolation Attempt at close interpersonal relationships and work on the ability to form an intimate relationship.
Stage 7--Middle Adulthood (40-60)	Generativity vs. stagnation Work at contributing to the personal and social process while dealing with changes in relationships/professional life. Exhibits a willingness to help others through empathy skills.
Stage 8--Late Adulthood (60-beyond)	Integrity vs. despair Introspective, questioning the importance of life, Was life worthwhile or a failure?

The personality issues that often emerge in the experiential group experience seem to have many of their origins in the Erikson psycho/social development process. This particular model of Erikson's can be used effectively as a theoretical guide for developing insights into possible explanations of psychological symptoms, such as alcohol and drug abuse, chronic anger, depression, anxiety, food abuse, interpersonal difficulties, shyness, self-destructions, etc. The reflective nature of this theory can and does often serves as the insight catalyst for personal awareness and possible behavior change.

Along with the Erikson model, the work of Daniel Levinson (1978) can be very helpful to group members to understand critical life issues. The Levinson model uses a language style that is very easy to understand. The major components of the Levinson developmental stages are as follows:

I. Early Adult Transition (17-22)
    A. Tasks
        1. Terminate the adolescent life structure
        2. Initiate movement into the adult world
    B. Typical Issues
        1. Independence from parents
        2. Supporting self
        3. Increasing psychological distance from family
        4. Learning about self and the world
        5. Articulating an appealing set of hopes for adulthood
        6. Taking responsibility
    C. Ends when one achieves psychological independence from family of origin

II. Entering the Adult World (22-28)
   A. Tasks
      1. Explore alternative options while avoiding strong commitments
      2. Create a stable (but provisional) life structure
   B. Typical Issues
      1. Supporting self and family
      2. Defining a career
      3. Finding the right mate
      4. Formulating ambitions
      5. Taking shallow roots
      6. Dividing time between family and job
      7. Adjusting core values to job demands
      8. Passing for an adult
   C. Ends when the strengthening need is to get beyond the provisional commitments as this stage becomes undeniable
III. The Age 30 transition (28-33)
   A. Tasks
      1. Reappraisal and termination of provisional, early adult life styles
      2. Initiation of choices leading to more stability
   B. Typical Issues
      1. Sense of urgency about making or remaking choices before its too late
      2. Give "dreams" a chance
      3. Regain integrity
      4. Emotional crisis
      5. Getting serious
      6. Avoiding inadequate commitments

    C. Ends when termination of provisional structure is complete and movement toward a revised or reaffirmed life structure is undertaken

IV. Settling Down (33-40)

    A. Early Tasks (33-36)

        1. Establish stable life structure

        2. Identify and plan for accomplishment of long-term goals

        3. Work at advancement (fulfill the dream)

    B. Late Tasks (36-40)

        1. Continue to work at advancement

        2. Achieve full adulthood in career

    C. Typical Issues

        1. Climbing the ladder of success

        2. Autonomy

        3. Gaining respect and admiration

        4. Accomplishments

        5. Becoming your own person

        6. Being a leader instead of a technician

    D. Ends when one pauses to appraise accomplishments of the period in light of increasing age and the awareness of not attaining every goal

V. Midlife Transition (40-45)

    A. Tasks

        1. Terminate early adulthood structure

        2. Redefine self and dream for the second half of life

        3. Initiate modification or replacement of old structure

    B. Typical Issues

        1. Is success worth the sacrifices?

        2. What's happened to the family?

3. Was the dream impossible from the start?
4. Am I responsible for my situation?
5. My friends are dying!
6. Is this all there is?
7. Am I really this old?
8. Can I become closer to people?
9. What can I do before I die?
10. What should I do about my parents?
11. How can I be the person I want to be?
C. Ends when steps are initiated toward a middle adulthood life structure
VI. Entering Middle Adulthood (45-50)
   A. Tasks
      1. Create a satisfactory life structure for middle adulthood
   B. Typical Issues
      1. Redefining success
      2. Worry about parents
      3. Responsibility

Both the Erikson and Levinson developmental stages can be used as part of a mini-lecturette. Not only do these theories help in the understanding of the phases in personal development, they are helpful for group dynamics members in their analytical work as they try to get insights into the workings of the group process.

Chapter 10

EXPERIENTIAL GROUP INTERACTION

For the experiential group to be effective, the group interaction should be balanced with nearly all members participating. Since the goal of the experiential group is improvement in terms of adaptive behavior, it is hoped that some parts of the group sessions would be devoted to the consideration of a troubled group member by the other group members. If empathy skills can be properly developed in the earlier structured group sessions, there is a strong likelihood that the group members will have the interest as well as the ability to deal with the verbal interaction required for the focus on a particular member's concerns.

Again the emphasis should be focused on the "here and now," and not on the member's past. By concentrating on the current concerns, the group member gets the opportunity for the group feedback, and, hopefully, insights into personal behavior.

In experiential groups there are members who will not discuss their own feelings and in no way show themselves. They are often just content to be a quiet group member involved in the exchange of reasonably nonthreatening material. For the group leader to feel like something is developing, it is important to utilize the structured exercises and supporting theory to get the quiet member to move on to a higher level of interaction.

On the other extreme, there are group members who spend considerable time talking about their concerns. The group leader's skills are often needed here. In many cases the assertive person does not want help and is presenting material to dominate or challenge the other group members. Often group members will react to the assertive members with their own assertive style, and the net result turns out to be nothing more than a gripe session. Confrontation between members can be very helpful toward self-understanding if it is not of the fault finding/attacking gripe session variety. Confrontive behavior is often anxiety producing, not only for the confronter and confrontee, but for the rest of the group. If the group members have learned to face each other with empathetic responses to concerns of one another, then they are well on the road to more effective human interaction. It must be remembered that fault finding and attacking is not confrontation and is far removed from the empathetic skills that are needed for self-understanding.

Chapter 11

EVALUATING THE EXPERIENTIAL GROUP EXPERIENCE

Jacob Klapman (1959) suggests that the benefits derived from participation in group might be evident in the following:
1. increased spontaneity,
2. greater group participation,
3. cultural adjustment,
4. disappearance of some maladaptive behavior,
5. disappearance of negativism,
6. apparent conflict reduction, and
7. the group members own statement about the help they have received.

Experiential groups lend themselves by nature to be evaluated by the progress made by the individual group members. I would like to add some of the group dynamics class evaluations that I have received as support for participating in a group experience.

(Student 1) This group dynamics class has really opened my eyes to some new concepts and ideas. It made me change the way I look at people and things. Now when I see someone acting in an odd way, I wonder why. My mind tends to wander back to the group dynamics class experience when we discussed types of maladaptive behavior. The group experience made me interested in people and their behavioral patterns.

(Student 2) The group experience affected me personally. I learned that a lot of my habits that I thought were normal are not. The group made me aware that I have the tendency to overreact a little too much. I now try to stop myself from acting this way. After thinking situations out, I usually find they aren't as bad as I made them out to be. I know I feel better about a lot of things and find myself worrying about a lot less.

(Student 3) I like the way the group was run. The sessions were always interesting and led to personal thought and involvement. This allowed us to learn more about our own behavior, and allowed us to open up to new things. I think the most important thing I learned in the group experience is that even though people act differently, they are still people and cannot control their problems. I learned to be open to more things and maybe this will help me to accept more people for who they are.

(Student 4)   After my completion of the group dynamics class I began to search for my own definitions of me. I looked for things that made me happy. I began to define goals that would make me feel accomplished, rather than constantly seeking the praise from another. I began the quest of learning to enjoy people, rather than to stay distant for fear that they would betray me or hurt me in some other way. I learned to let go of my excuses, legitimate or otherwise, for not having the life that I wanted or at least pursuing it. I learned that when I didn't get the things that I thought that I should have that all I can do is try to understand why, learn how to do it better next time if that opportunity approaches, and enjoy the fact that I had the opportunity in the first place. I learned that life is balanced.

Chapter 12

EXPERIENTIAL GROUP CONTRACT

Everett Shostrom (1969) suggests that the following information be made available to all participants:

1. an explicit statement of the purpose of the group,
2. education and the training of the group leader,
3. goals of the group experience and activities/techniques to be used,
4. amounts and kinds of responsibility to be assumed by the group leader and by the group members,
5. issues of confidentiality, and
6. if the purpose is primarily educational, the group leader assumes the professional and ethical obligations of an educator.

For the college professor conducting a group dynamics class the syllabus becomes the contractual statement. I have included the following suggestions for use in syllabus development.

COURSE DESCRIPTION: Group Dynamics is a course designed to introduce students to the experiential group dynamics process. An experiential group's primary focus is on developing a student's understanding of group-level processes and of his or her own behavior in groups. The method is essentially inductive, moving from specific group experiences to general ideas about group processes. By drawing on their own resources, students attempt to come to terms with the task of becoming a group and increasing their understanding of group processes.

COURSE FORMAT: The group dynamics course is organized around the phases in group development. The framework provides an order to topics addressed in readings, paper assignments, and the experiential group sessions. The course will have a clearly defined beginning and ending, but as with any reasonable notion of developmental phases, there may not be a sharp or unequivocal movement from one phase to the next.

CLASS ATTENDANCE: Class attendance is required of all class sessions (experiential group) barring personal emergency (defined as serious illness, family crisis, or unavoidable accident). The theoretical point on attendance is that without the mandatory attendance rule, the group process would not become strong enough for learning to occur. Each experiential group session that is missed will result in the lowering of the letter grade. (one missed group session= B, two missed group sessions=C, etc.)

EVALUATION AND WRITING ASSIGNMENTS: Student behavior in the experiential group sessions will not be used as a basis for grades. Grades will not be helped nor hurt by how much or how little students talk. Two written papers (3-5 pages in length) turned in during the course of the seminar will be the sole basis for grades with the exception of the mandatory attendance requirement. The papers are to relate to events from the group sessions as well as concepts from the text and readings. In each paper students describe thoroughly and accurately what occurred during the group sessions and then analyze these events as they relate to the phases of group development. Students are encouraged to keep journals of their experiences with the course for reviewing their own feelings and fantasies. This will help them keep much of the necessary data for their analysis papers. The journal will not be turned in for any type of evaluation.

Chapter 13

A FINAL NOTE

Today groups are seen in operation is all walks of life. It seems that any organization or business that wishes to appear progressive adopts some form of a group process.

There are many approaches to the group process. Each of these approaches are accompanied by interesting testimonies, and each theorist would appear to have a good theoretical justification for the approach used.

From my own experience, I have found some definite components that are necessary for a successful group experience. The single most important skill for the group leader is the ability to have well-developed empathy skills. Carl Rogers (1969) in his concept of active listening sets the stage, especially in the beginning sessions, for giving and receiving feedback. Without developing this skill, the group leader will have an almost impossible task in developing the group process.

The use of techniques and exercises are of critical importance. I like to start with the least threatening exercises (well-structured for group security and well-being) and then proceed to the point where the group can generate its own agenda.

I hope that the group movement can continue to develop and find a comfortable niche in which to operate. By utilizing well-established group process theories, the experiential group process can be a valuable tool in creating a positive personal and societal change.

Alderfer, Clayton (1995). "Conditions for Teaching
    Experiential Group Dynamics." in Gillette and
    McCollom (eds.). Groups in Context. Lanham,
    Md.:University Press of America.

Bennis and Shephard (1956). "A Theory of Group
    Development." Human Relations, Vol 9.

Bion, W. R. (1963). Experiences in Group. New
    York:Basic Books.

_____(1965). Learning from Experience. New
    York:Basic Books.

Corsini and Rosenberg (1955). "Mechanisms of Group
    Psychotherapy: Processes and Dynamics." Journal
    of Abnormal and Social Psychology, Vol. 15.

Erikson, Eric (1963). Childhood and Society. New
    York:Norton.

Foulkes, S. H. (1949). Introduction to Group
    Psychotherapy. New York: Grune and Stratton.

Hare and Bales (1963). "Seating Position and Small Group
    Interaction." Sociometry, Vol. 26.

Hovland, Janis and Kelley (1953). Communication and
    Persuasion. New Haven:Yale University Press.

Johnson, James H. (1963). Group Therapy: A Practical
    Approach. New York: McGraw-Hill.

Klapman, J. W. (1959). Group Psychotherapy: Theory and Practice. New York:Grune and Stratton.

Leopold, H. S. (1957). "Selection of Patients for Group Psychotherapy." American Journal of Psychotherapy, Vol. 11.

Levinson, D. J. (1978). The Seasons of a Man's Life. New York: Ballantine Books.

Lewin, Kurt (1935). A Dynamic Theory of Personality. New York: McGraw-Hill.

_____(1948). Resolving Social Conflicts. New York: Harper.

Lifton, Walter (1961). Working with Groups. New York:Wiley.

Martin and Hill (1957). "Toward a Theory of Group Development: Six Phases of Therapy Group Development." International Journal of Group Psychotherapy, Vol. 7.

Mintz, E. E. (1967). "Time Extended Marathon Groups." Psychotherapy: Theory, Research, and Practice, Vol. 4.

Rogers, C. (1969). "The Group Comes of Age." Psychology Today, December.

Shostrom, E. (1969). "Group Therapy: Let the Buyer
    Beware." Psychology Today, May.

_____(1977). Actualizing Therapy. San Diego,
    Calif. EDS.

Thelen and Dickerman (1949). "Stereotypes and the
    Growth of Groups." Educational Leadership,
    February.

Yalom, Irvin (1966). "A Study of Group Therapy
    Dropouts." Archives of General Psychiatry, Vol. 4.